9/93

S0-AAD-530

THE MOON OF THE
OWLS

THE THIRTEEN MOONS

The Moon of the Owls (JANUARY)

The Moon of the Bears (FEBRUARY)

The Moon of the Salamanders (MARCH)

The Moon of the Chickarees (APRIL)

The Moon of the Monarch Butterflies (MAY)

The Moon of the Fox Pups (JUNE)

The Moon of the Wild Pigs (JULY)

The Moon of the Mountain Lions (AUGUST)

The Moon of the Deer (SEPTEMBER)

The Moon of the Alligators (OCTOBER)

The Moon of the Gray Wolves (NOVEMBER)

The Moon of the Winter Bird (DECEMBER)

The Moon of the Moles (DECEMBER-JANUARY)

NEW EDITION   THE THIRTEEN MOONS

THE MOON OF THE
OWLS

BY JEAN CRAIGHEAD GEORGE

ILLUSTRATED BY WENDELL MINOR

HarperCollins*Publishers*

The illustrations in this book were
painted with gouache and watercolor
on number 80, cold-press finish,
bainbridge board.

The Moon of the Owls
Text copyright © 1967, 1993 by Jean Craighead George
Illustrations copyright © 1993 by Wendell Minor
 Printed in the United States of America. For
information address HarperCollins Children's Books, a division of
HarperCollins Publishers, 10 East 53rd Street, New York, NY 10022.
Published simultaneously in Canada by HarperCollins
Publishers Ltd.
Typography by Al Cetta
1 2 3 4 5 6 7 8 9 10
NEW EDITION

Library of Congress Cataloging-in-Publication Data
George, Jean Craighead, date
    The moon of the owls / by Jean Craighead George ; illustrated
by Wendell Minor.—New ed.
        p.   cm. — (The Thirteen moons)
    Summary: A great horned owl's stirrings to mate carry him
across a forest in January in the Catskill Mountains, where he
observes the nocturnal activities of other animals.
        ISBN 0-06-020192-4. — ISBN 0-06-020193-2 (lib. bdg.)
    1. Owls—Juvenile literature.   2. Great horned owl—New
York (State)—Catskill Mountains—Juvenile literature.   [1. Great
horned owl.   2. Owl.   3. Animals.   4. Night.]   I. Minor,
Wendell, ill.   II. Series: George Jean Craighead, date, Thirteen
moons (HarperCollins)
QL795.B57G38   1993   91-2735
598'.97—dc20   CIP
                                                                         AC

Why is this series called The Thirteen Moons?

Each year there are either thirteen full moons or thirteen new moons. This series of books is named in their honor.

Our culture, which bases its calendar year on sun-time, has no names for the thirteen moons. I have named the thirteen lunar months after thirteen North American animals. Primarily night prowlers, these animals, at a particular time of the year in a particular place, do wondrous things. The places are known to you, but the animal moon names are not because I made them up. So that you can place them on our sun calendar, I have identified them with the names of our months. When I ran out of these, I gave the thirteenth moon, the Moon of the Moles, the expandable name December-January.

Fortunately, the animals do not need calendars, for names or no names, sun-time or moon-time, they follow their own inner clocks.

—JEAN CRAIGHEAD GEORGE

THE FULL MOON OF JANUARY rose into the stars. Its pale light shone down on the rolling Catskill Mountains in New York and turned the bare trees silver. A newly fallen snow glowed blue. The needles on a pine tree gleamed like glassy spears. They cast their pointed shadows on a great horned owl sitting on a limb against the trunk. He had just opened his large lemon-yellow eyes and was staring into the moonlit woods.

It was January, the moon of beginnings. From coast to coast, from Canada through Mexico, the great horned owl is the bold living symbol of this moon. Like the ancient Roman god Janus, for whom January is named, the great horned owl opens the door to all beginnings.

The owl, who stood almost two feet high, stared into the sunless forest. To him there was no darkness. The pale light from the moon and stars, and their reflections off the snow and clouds, fell onto mirrorlike cells on the retina of his eyes. The cells magnified the dim light, and he could see even though it was dark. He saw a snowflake on his great hooked beak. He saw a twig fall from the pine. Through these eyes, and his unique ears, the night is day.

The great horned owl is a magnificent bird of prey with tan and brown feathers, feet that are as

big as baseballs, and heavy talons as sharp as darning needles. His wingspread is four feet from tip to tip.

He stood tall in the pine tree. He pulsated the large patch of white feathers under his beak as he came awake in the roost tree. He had slept here almost every day for eight years. His reddish facial disc, rimmed with jet-black feathers, caught specks of starlight and directed them into his eyes. He lowered, then raised, the two earlike tufts on his head that gave him the name "cat owl." He was not trying to hear better, for his ears were lower on his head, but to look more like the stub of a tree.

The owl was large and grand, the winged tiger of the woods who, on this night, would throw open the door to spring. He blinked. No birds sang, no insects strummed. The frogs and toads were silent. It was a frigid January night in the Northern Hemisphere.

He circled his head almost completely around to his back as he surveyed his land. He did not see the woodchuck or the bear. The bats were either far to the south or hanging upside down in hollow trees and in caves. Their bodies would be cold, their hearts beating very slowly. They would breathe but twice in fifteen minutes. The season of hibernation was still upon the land.

And yet the forest was not still. The deer and foxes were walking in the moonlight. Mice were tunneling under the snow, and minks and weasels were sliding down riverbanks.

The owl lifted one of his flight feathers and ran his beak down the shaft to groom it. It snapped back into place without making a sound. Wisps of down grow along the edges of owl feathers and mute the rustling sound of their wings. When he flies, he travels as silently as a falling star.

The owl looked down on his six square miles of property in the Catskills, a combination of forest, fields, and swamps. On his western boundary rose a dark cliff. Over this landmark in autumn he and his much larger mate would chase their young of the year, sending them off to find their own homes, perhaps taking the place of a bird that had died. The old pair would also chase away other young of their kind who were looking for homes. They would not tolerate any other member of their species on their territory. It was to them food, shelter, and a nesting site for their young.

Suddenly the owl bobbed his head in excitement. This moon bespoke a dramatic beginning. He did not know why, but he wanted to be on the move this night. He opened his wings and flew.

He soared silently down the mountain, speeding between the tree limbs. Miraculously, he avoided every twig. He came to rest on a pine beside the "small-bird tree," where many of the daytime birds slept. The tree was an old beech with pale dry leaves that clung to it all winter. The little birds—cardinals, juncos, and finches—roosted among the leaves. Their body heat reflected off the leaves, making the space around each bird a warm little microclimate.

The big owl did not see the birds, for they were sitting perfectly still. Then a cardinal pulled one cold foot up into his feathers and put the warmed one down. Because of that movement, the owl saw the little bird. He did not catch it. His food was bigger game: rabbits, squirrels, skunks, porcupines. For the most part he left the little birds and mice to the smaller owls, the saw-whet,

who had come down from Canada for the winter, and the screech owl.

The great horned owl lifted his feathers and shook. He fluttered his white beard in excitement. Not because the pesky blue jay who screamed at him during the day was sleeping below him, not because the nuthatch had awakened in his tree hole and was leaning out to check the cold, and not because the sparrows and the juncos were striking their bodies with closed wings to keep themselves warm. He was responding to an exuberance within him.

He sailed off and, without making a sound, alighted on his favorite maple tree on the stream bank near an open field. He swung his head and glanced around. Nothing was moving, but he could hear tiny feet pattering. Now his eyes and ears worked together to pinpoint the sound with a three-point fix. The sound came from the empty crow's nest in the Scotch pine tree. The crows who chased and screamed at him during the day were roosting in a grove of pines ten miles away with hundreds of their kind. Yet the owl had seen their stick nest move. He focused his eyes acutely. A white-footed deer mouse who had taken up residence in the nest for the winter was getting up. The owl focused on the mouse with his fovea, an area of acute vision near the bottom of his eye. Another fovea at the top of his eye gave him acute vision in another direction. This dynamic winged tiger had keen vision up, down, and straight ahead, all at the same time. Although he was not above eating a white-footed deer mouse, the owl ignored the mouse. The call of his mission was greater than his hunger.

Bubbles moved under the ice in the stream

below him. A mink was blowing air from his nose as he swam under the water. The bubbles flowed down his whiskers and over his back, turning his brown fur silver. He plunged over a sunken log and disappeared into darkness.

Presently he came up, slipped through a hole in the ice, and bounced ashore with a sunfish in his mouth. He put it down and shook his water-repellent guard hairs. Almost instantly they were dry.

The owl did not strike the mink. He knew the animal was as powerful as himself. Curiously he turned his head upside down and watched the handsome mink in the top fovea of his eye, then righted his head and watched him in the lower fovea. The mink ate his fish and dove for another. The owl felt the night calling to him and looked toward his cliff.

Under the water the mink swam past the larva of a caddis fly. The wormlike animal lived inside a chimney he had built of tiny sand grains. The front door, a silken mat on a hinge, opened, and he leaned out and held his net of feathery mouth parts in the current. When he had collected several one-celled animals, he pulled himself inside, closed his door, and sorted the food from the silt. Then he opened his door and threw out the refuse, closed it once again, and ate.

A water spider under the stream sat inside an air-filled diving bell she had made with her silk and an empty snail shell. Here in her bubble of air in the warm water she would live through the snow and freezing temperatures that killed most land spiders. She was quiet, barely breathing. The mink swam past her, came ashore, and dived into the snow. He burst to the surface at the top of a rise, rolled, then slid downhill to his den. Well fed and well exercised, he entered his labyrinth through a hole under a rock and loped off to his bedroom among the roots of the forest plants.

The owl flew on with sudden urgency. He soared over an empty vireo nest and past the limb where the flycatcher sat in summer to wait for insects. The bird was in South America, but the limb was not deserted. Under the bark were the eggs of a cucujid beetle that had been deliberately laid beside the eggs of a bark beetle. The cucujids would hatch before the bark beetles and, as their mother had planned, the hatchlings would eat them. A few of the bark beetle eggs would survive, hatch, and burrow under the bark. The limb of the tree would die, and upon her return in May the flycatcher would eat both kinds of beetles as they matured and flew off.

The owl pumped his wings and climbed above the forest canopy, then soared down to a willow tree at the edge of his marsh. It was two o'clock— the coldest hour of the January moon.

He folded his wings and unfolded them high above his head. His white throat patch thumped. Energy surged through him, then died. He sat quietly.

Presently he noticed the beaver pond. Under the ice a beaver with an aspen log in his mouth was laboriously swimming, using his feet and steering with his tail. He emerged near his lodge and, bracing himself with his tail and feet, pulled the log with his teeth. He had cut it last summer and poked it into the mud to preserve it for the winter famine. Carefully he worked the end of the log up a watery tunnel and into his dry lodge. Here there was a room with reeds for a floor and

mud and sticks for walls. His mate and his large son of the year helped pull the log into their home. They ate the bark only, gnawing and rotating the log as if it were an ear of corn.

When the owl could no longer see the beaver, he studied the marsh. A reed quivered, cracked, and fell. A muskrat emerged beside it. Muskrat was reliable owl food. Muskrats were active in spring, summer, winter, and autumn. The owl was contemplating taking the food when the surge of energy rushed through his body again, and he lifted and folded his wings.

He flew on to his oak tree above the marsh and the beaver pond, where he could see the cliff. He lifted himself into the air and dropped back onto the limb. January was speaking to him.

He took to his wings again, beating his way toward the cliff. He went over the rocky hillside where the black snakes slept. He did not see them, for they were under the logs and snow, wound around each other like threads in a ball of yarn.

The owl coasted over a hollow log where a mother skunk slept with her four youngsters of the past year. Skunks were a favorite great horned owl food despite the dousing of musk they gave off when caught. Nothing stirred at the skunk den.

He flew on, passing a porcupine curled up against the cold in a hollow tree. The porcupine instinctively knew that it was dangerous to sleep in a forest where great horned owls, gray foxes, Canada lynx, and eastern coyotes hunted. He had gone to sleep with his quills facing outward. An enemy would get a faceful of quills if it tried to pull him out. This had happened to one of the great horned owl's past mates, and she had not survived the relentless migration of the quills through her body.

Below the porcupine's tree a cluster of snow fleas was gathered. Their eyes glittered, but they did not move, for the air was too cold. They were waiting for daylight, when reflected heat from the sun would bounce off the snow and warm them. They would then thump their long slender legs and sail three feet into the air. When they fell back, they would thump and go up again. In this manner they danced the snow-flea courtship hop until the sun moved and they grew cold again.

Well past the porcupine and the snow fleas, the owl pressed harder on his wings and flew faster. He had seen a great horned owl, even larger than himself, skimming above the cliff. The other owl did not provoke him to chase, but to veer off to the pine grove and drop to his stick nest. It had

once been a crow's nest, which he and his new mate of four years ago had taken over.

The owl picked up a stick in his beak. His throat quivered as the stick stirred memories of eggs and young. He lifted his wings and snapped his beak with a loud crack.

Flapping his wings, he shook off fine bits of fuzz from his feathers. He shook again. More fuzz floated away on the cold air. When he folded his wings to his body, he was more brilliant in color, more regal and spectacular. The moon of January was beginning the beginning.

A starling in an abandoned woodpecker hole scratched in his sleep and dislodged a feather. A brighter feather would grow in its place. The longer hours of daylight were bringing the plumage of the birds into breeding condition. Some, like the owl, sloughed off dull ends and became

bright and vivid; others, like the starling, grew colorful new feathers.

The owl flew to the edge of a field. Something was moving. His keen eyes came into focus on the snow. It was the weasel. She was in her winter coat—all white, except her nose and black tail tip. She dove and leaped. She rolled on her back, flipped to her feet, and tunneled around a goldenrod stalk. She was not hunting on this night of the January full moon—she was playing. She was still a youngster from the past year.

A twig snapped and a red fox seemed to float into the field. His fur was loose and clean from the snow. He lifted his paw and bit the ice that had frozen between his toes. More comfortable now, he listened and stalked. Throwing his ears forward, he gracefully pounced on a covey of seven quail sleeping in a circle, heads out, to watch for danger. They burst out of the snow in all directions like fire bits from a sparkler. The agile fox walked away with one in his mouth.

A cottontail rabbit was bedded down in a cup of snow. She ran wildly before her enemy, the fox, and frightened a mouse, who skittered over the top of the snow. A screech owl plunged and caught the mouse. Then she flew back to the stub upon which she did all her hunting and eating. She swallowed the mouse whole. In the manner of all birds of prey, the great horned owl included, she would regurgitate a pellet of the indigestible fur and bones from her stomach sometime the next night before eating again.

The great horned owl shifted his gaze from the dramas below and watched the cliff. He looked away, then swung his head from side to side and bobbed it up and down excitedly. He had caught sight of the terrified rabbit as she flattened her ears to her head. Now she was still and the owl lost sight of her. By not moving, rabbits hide from their enemies.

The cottontail was alone, as were all the other members of her family. Over the ages they had evolved a system to protect themselves. By scattering, they made it more difficult for enemies to find them.

No longer seeing the rabbit, the owl flew on toward the cliff. He alighted on the top of one of the oldest trees in his territory, a whispering hemlock whose graceful needles cast shadows of lace on the snow.

Something moved near the tree's base. The owl dropped to a lower limb to see if this could be the source of his excitement, and looked into the large eyes of a white-tailed deer. She was standing

alone. She was pregnant. Six and a half months from October, when she had mated, her fawn would be born. The baby would arrive when the tender spring leaves of the flowers and grasses were abundant.

The doe had been under the hemlock since sunset. All week she had browsed the dogwood and birch twigs with her herd in the valley, where they had gathered for the winter. Just before the sun had set, she had felt her fawn stir within her. Turning away from the herd, she had climbed the hill looking under every oak and beech tree along the way. At last she had come to the ancient hemlock. She butted its branches that reached to the ground and trampled the snow beneath it. Then she lay down. Limbs drooped around her; she could barely see the forest. Nothing, she sensed, could see her. She put her long slender

nose on her shoulder and rested a moment. Then she got up and walked back to the herd. She had found a place to give birth to her fawn. She would come back to this place many times before it was born.

The owl preened his feathers. He strutted along the limb. The doe was gnawing the lichens on the side of a poplar tree. She pulled down the twigs of a beech tree and ate them. Like the mice, the beaver, and the rabbits, the doe could find little green food in January.

Suddenly the winged tiger rose up off the limb and fell softly back. He pivoted and bowed. This dance had opened the door; the beginning was moving on.

"WHO WHOWHO, WHO WHO," he boomed. His white throat throbbed. His ear tufts sat straight up. "WHO WHOWHO, WHO

WHO." His resonant voice was like a foghorn in the night.

"Who, whowho, who who." His mate answered from the cliff area, where she had wintered alone.

The owl spread his wings, flew over the treetops, the frozen waterfalls, the sleeping and active animals, and arrived at the cliff. He alighted beside his mate.

At dawn the Northern Hemisphere looked no different from the day before. And yet those haunting calls in the night had changed it all. The great horned owl had opened the door to the beginning of new life in the woods. The annual courtship of the great horned owls had begun.

Bibliography

Brady, Irene. *Owlet, the Great Horned Owl*. Boston: Houghton Mifflin, 1974.

Craighead, Frank and John. *Hawks in the Hand*. Boston: Houghton Mifflin, 1939.

Everett, Michael. *A Natural History of Owls*. London, New York: Hamlyn, 1977.

Garelick, May. *About Owls*. New York: Four Winds, 1975.

Hoke, Helen. *Owls*. New York: F. Watts, 1974.

Lavine, Sigmund A. *Wonders of the Owl World*. New York: Dodd, Mead, 1971.

National Geographic Society. *Field Guide to the Birds of North America*. Washington, D.C.: 1987.

Storm, Laura. *The Owl Book*. Minneapolis: Lerner, 1983.

Walker, Lewis Wayne. *The Book of Owls*. New York: Knopf, 1974.

Index